ANGRY BIRDS™
PLAYGROUND
ATLAS

ANGRY BIRDS

PLAYGROUND

ATLAS

BY ELIZABETH CARNEY

NATIONAL
GEOGRAPHIC
Washington, D.C.

CONTINENTS OF THE WORLD

NORTH AMERICA

EUROPE

ASIA

AFRICA

SOUTH AMERICA

AUSTRALIA

ANTARCTICA

Key to the Maps

⊛ Country capital

⊙ Other capital

• City

∴ Ruin

◆ Research station

········· Boundary

Ice cap

Tundra

Grassland

Desert

Wetland

Coniferous forest

Deciduous forest

Rain forest

Mountain

Contents

AN ATLAS IS A BOOK OF MAPS. MAPS ARE DRAWINGS OF PLACES AS THEY APPEAR FROM ABOVE. THERE ARE PICTURES OF PEOPLE, PLACES, AND THINGS THAT WE CAN FIND THERE.

THIS ATLAS HAS MAPS OF THE WORLD'S CONTINENTS. A CONTINENT IS A BIG DIVISION OF LAND ON EARTH. THERE ARE SEVEN CONTINENTS: NORTH AMERICA, SOUTH AMERICA, EUROPE, AFRICA, ASIA, AUSTRALIA, AND ANTARCTICA.

9

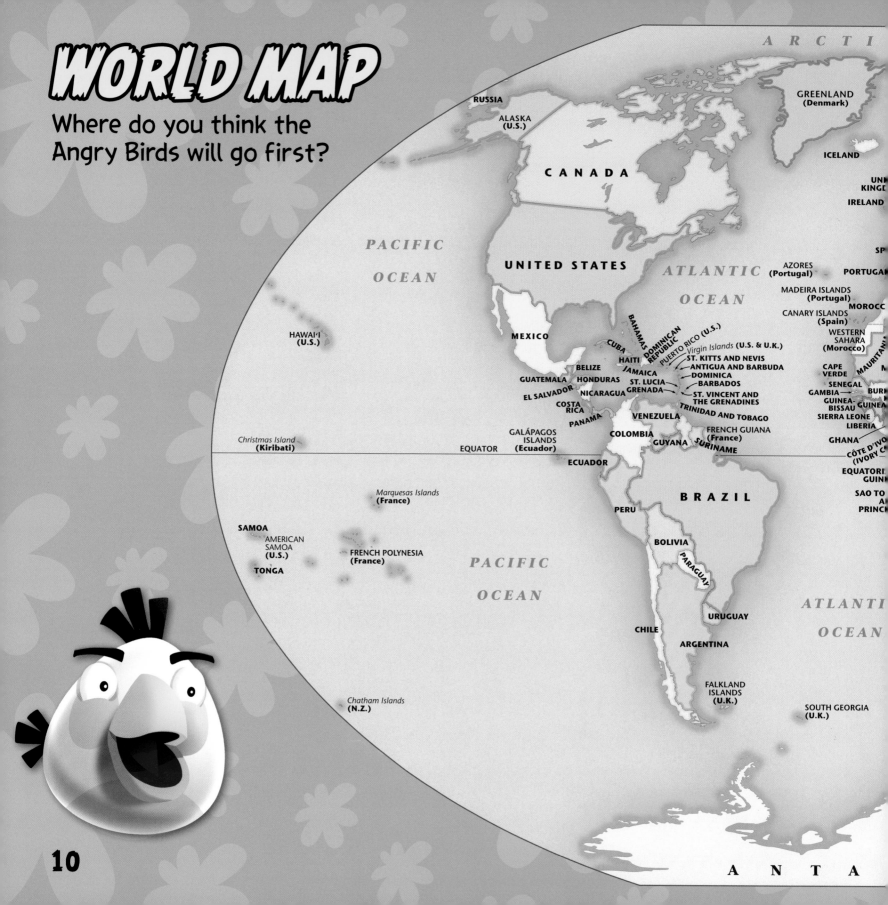

WORLD MAP

Where do you think the
Angry Birds will go first?

ARCTI

RUSSIA

ALASKA
(U.S.)

GREENLAND
(Denmark)

ICELAND

CANADA

UNI
KINGD

IRELAND

PACIFIC

OCEAN

UNITED STATES

ATLANTIC

OCEAN

AZORES
(Portugal)

SP

PORTUGA

MADEIRA ISLANDS
(Portugal)

MOROCC

CANARY ISLANDS
(Spain)

HAWAI'I
(U.S.)

MEXICO

BAHAMAS

CUBA

DOMINICAN
REPUBLIC

PUERTO RICO (U.S.)

Virgin Islands (U.S. & U.K.)

ST. KITTS AND NEVIS

WESTERN
SAHARA
(Morocco)

MAURITANIA

HAITI

JAMAICA

BELIZE

GUATEMALA   HONDURAS

ANTIGUA AND BARBUDA

DOMINICA

BARBADOS

CAPE
VERDE

SENEGAL

EL SALVADOR

ST. LUCIA

GRENADA

ST. VINCENT AND
THE GRENADINES

GAMBIA

GUINEA-
BISSAU

GUINEA

BUR

NICARAGUA

COSTA
RICA

PANAMA

VENEZUELA

TRINIDAD AND TOBAGO

SIERRA LEONE

LIBERIA

Christmas Island
(Kiribati)

GALÁPAGOS
ISLANDS
(Ecuador)

EQUATOR

COLOMBIA

GUYANA

FRENCH GUIANA
(France)

SURINAME

GHANA

CÔTE D'IVO
(IVORY C

ECUADOR

EQUATORI
GUIN

SAO TO
A
PRINC

Marquesas Islands
(France)

BRAZIL

SAMOA

PERU

AMERICAN
SAMOA
(U.S.)

FRENCH POLYNESIA
(France)

PACIFIC

OCEAN

BOLIVIA

PARAGUAY

ATLANTI

OCEAN

TONGA

URUGUAY

CHILE

ARGENTINA

Chatham Islands
(N.Z.)

FALKLAND
ISLANDS
(U.K.)

SOUTH GEORGIA
(U.K.)

ANTA

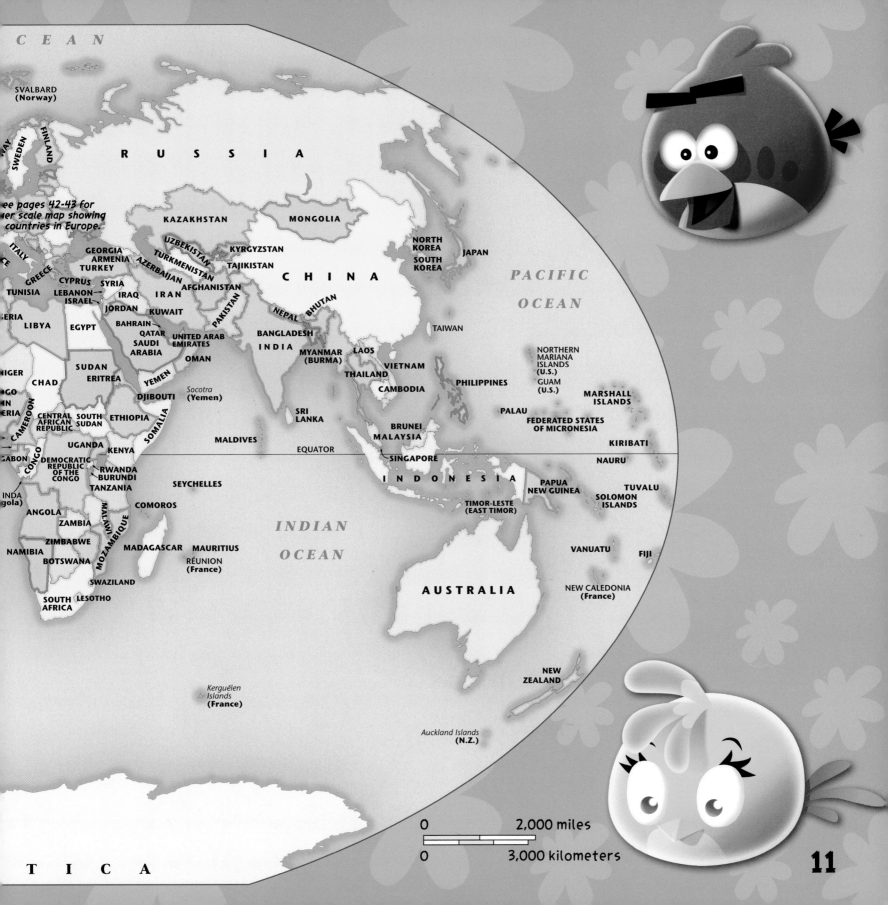

CEAN

SVALBARD
(Norway)

ee pages 42-43 for
er scale map showing
countries in Europe.

SWEDEN

FINLAND

R U S S I A

ITALY

GREECE

CYPRUS

TUNISIA

LEBANON
ISRAEL

GEORGIA
ARMENIA
TURKEY

AZERBAIJAN

SYRIA

IRAQ

IRAN

JORDAN

KUWAIT

KAZAKHSTAN

UZBEKISTAN

TURKMENISTAN

KYRGYZSTAN

TAJIKISTAN

AFGHANISTAN

MONGOLIA

NORTH
KOREA

SOUTH
KOREA

JAPAN

C H I N A

PACIFIC

OCEAN

LIBYA

EGYPT

BAHRAIN

QATAR

UNITED ARAB
EMIRATES

SAUDI
ARABIA

OMAN

PAKISTAN

NEPAL

BHUTAN

BANGLADESH

I N D I A

MYANMAR
(BURMA)

LAOS

TAIWAN

ERIA

NIGER

CHAD

SUDAN

ERITREA

YEMEN

DJIBOUTI

Socotra
(Yemen)

THAILAND

VIETNAM

CAMBODIA

NORTHERN
MARIANA
ISLANDS
(U.S.)

GUAM
(U.S.)

PHILIPPINES

MARSHALL
ISLANDS

GO

N

ERIA

CAMEROON

CENTRAL
AFRICAN
REPUBLIC

SOUTH
SUDAN

ETHIOPIA

SOMALIA

SRI
LANKA

PALAU

FEDERATED STATES
OF MICRONESIA

GABON

CONGO

DEMOCRATIC
REPUBLIC
OF THE
CONGO

UGANDA

RWANDA
BURUNDI

KENYA

TANZANIA

MALDIVES

EQUATOR

BRUNEI

MALAYSIA

SINGAPORE

I N D O N E S I A

PAPUA
NEW GUINEA

KIRIBATI

NAURU

TUVALU

SOLOMON
ISLANDS

INDA
gola)

ANGOLA

ZAMBIA

ZIMBABWE

MALAWI

MOZAMBIQUE

SEYCHELLES

COMOROS

MADAGASCAR

MAURITIUS

RÉUNION
(France)

I N D I A N

O C E A N

TIMOR-LESTE
(EAST TIMOR)

VANUATU

FIJI

NAMIBIA

BOTSWANA

SWAZILAND

SOUTH
AFRICA

LESOTHO

Kerguélen
Islands
(France)

A U S T R A L I A

NEW CALEDONIA
(France)

NEW
ZEALAND

Auckland Islands
(N.Z.)

0   2,000 miles

0   3,000 kilometers

TICA

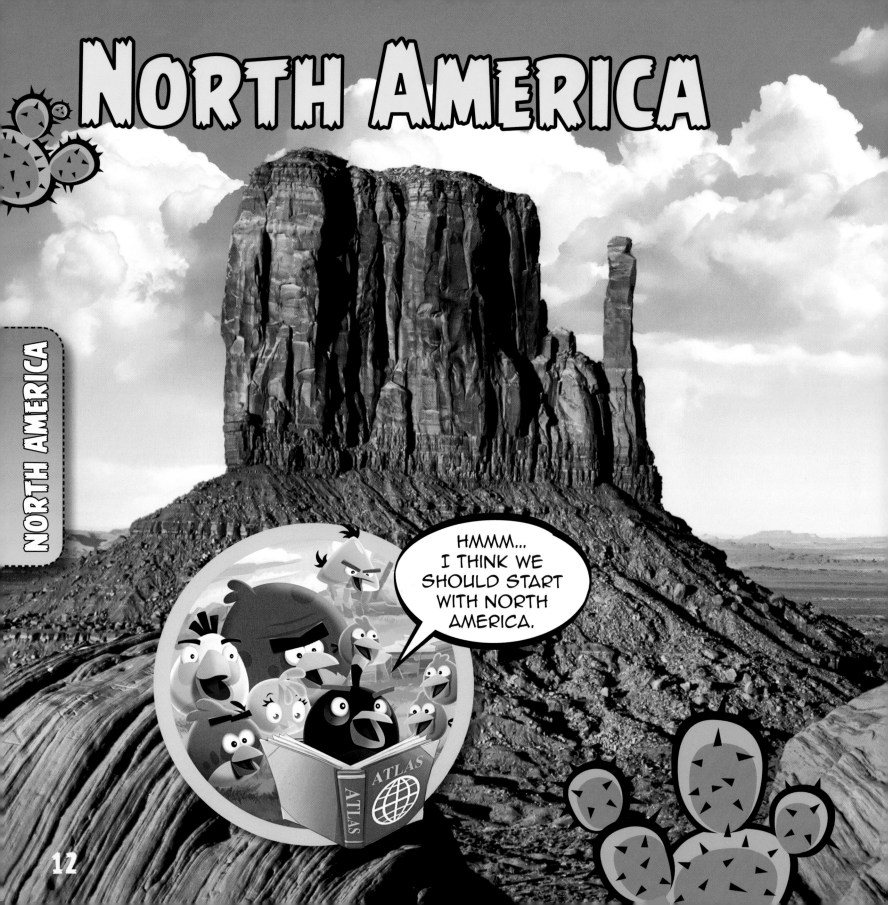

magine staring out the car window on a road trip from the northern to southern tip of North America. You could see nearly every type of environment on Earth. This continent has hot, rocky deserts and long mountain ranges. There are grassy plains and steamy rain forests. You'd even see ice fields and frozen land called tundra. North America has them all!

Arctic Ocean

NORTH AMERICA

EUROPE

ASIA

Atlantic Ocean

AFRICA

Pacific Ocean

SOUTH AMERICA

Indian Ocean

AUSTRALIA

ANTARCTICA

COUNTRIES OF NORTH AMERICA

NORTH AMERICA

There are 23 countries in North America. Canada, the United States, and Mexico are the largest. The continent includes the warm islands of the Caribbean. The seven countries that connect Mexico to South America make the southern tip. That area is sometimes called Central America.

Mexico City is the largest city in North America. Nearly nine million people live there. It's followed by New York and Los Angeles. Many cities are centers for making goods like cars and machines. Farming is very important, too. North America produces more of the world's food than any other continent.

CANADA AND THE U.S.A. ARE PRETTY BIG, LIKE TERENCE.

WOW, EACH COUNTRY IS A DIFFERENT SIZE!

COUNTRIES: 23

LARGEST COUNTRY: CANADA

SMALLEST COUNTRY: ST. KITTS AND NEVIS

LARGEST CITY: MEXICO CITY, MEXICO

FUN FACT: VIKING EXPLORER LEIF ERICSON FIRST SET FOOT IN NORTH AMERICA NEARLY 500 YEARS BEFORE CHRISTOPHER COLUMBUS!

North America is a place settled by people from other lands. Very long ago, people walked over a land bridge that connected Asia to North America. That bridge is gone now, but the descendants of these people, called Native Americans, are still here. They live all over North America, from snowy Canada to sunny Guatemala. In the 1500s and 1600s, settlers from Spain, England, and France began to arrive in North America. Some brought African slaves. Many people trace their roots back to these groups.

In more recent times, people from all over the world have made their homes in North America. North Americans celebrate their different cultures with festivals and parades. Sports are very popular. Football and baseball are two favorites!

GO, RED TEAM! GO!

IT LOOKS WARM IN GUATEMALA!

17

LAY OF THE LAND

Forests cover much of North America. In the mountains, pines and evergreens grow over snow-covered slopes. The Rocky Mountains stretch from Canada to Mexico. The Appalachians lie to the east. The land between them is mainly flat and great for farming. West of the Rockies, you'll find deserts dotted with canyons, cactus, and weirdly shaped rocks. Rivers and lakes provide an important source of water. In southern Mexico and Central America, desert gives way to green rain forests. Icy Greenland lies to the north. It's the world's largest island and is part of the country of Denmark.

HOT, DRY DESERTS IN THE WEST...

LOOK AT ALL THE KINDS OF LANDS IN NORTH AMERICA. TALL MOUNTAINS UP NORTH...

SIZE: 9,499,000 SQ MI (24,474,000 SQ KM)

HIGHEST PLACE: MOUNT McKINLEY, U.S.A.

LOWEST PLACE: DEATH VALLEY, U.S.A.

LONGEST RIVER: MISSISSIPPI RIVER, U.S.A.

FUN FACT: NORTH AMERICA'S MAMMOTH CAVE IN KENTUCKY, U.S.A., IS THE WORLD'S LARGEST CAVE SYSTEM.

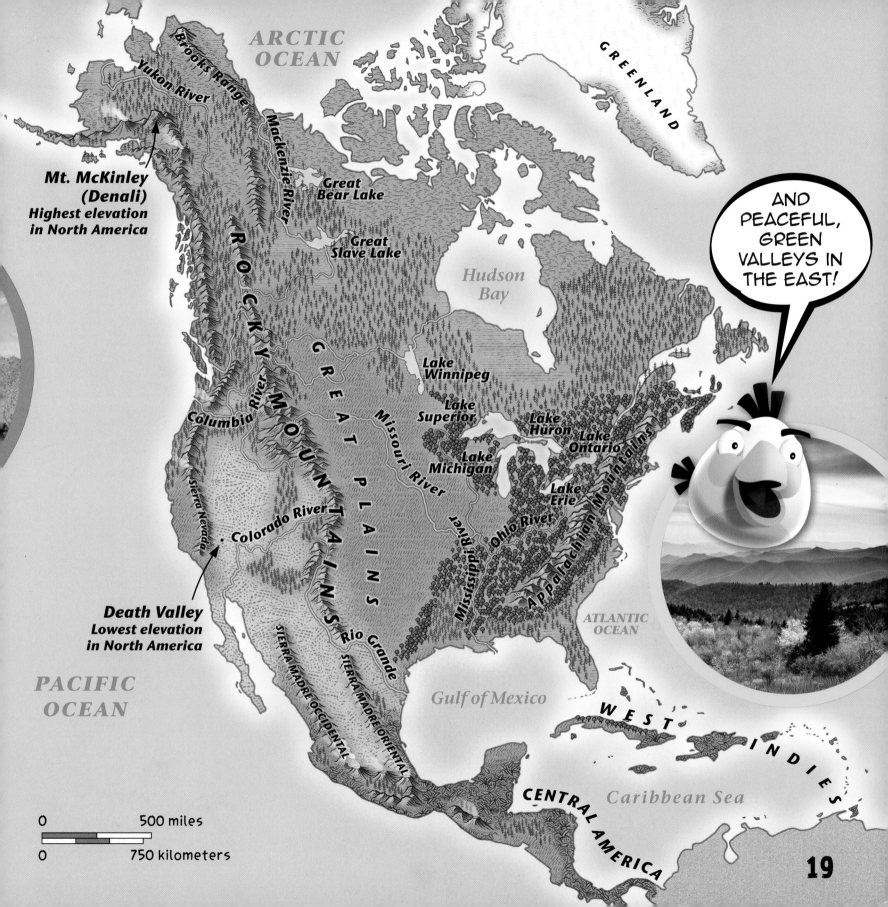

ARCTIC OCEAN

GREENLAND

Brooks Range

Yukon River

Mackenzie River

Mt. McKinley (Denali)
Highest elevation in North America

Great Bear Lake

Great Slave Lake

Hudson Bay

R O C K Y   M O U N T A I N S

G R E A T   P L A I N S

Columbia River

Sierra Nevada

Lake Winnipeg

Lake Superior

Lake Huron

Lake Michigan

Lake Ontario

Lake Erie

Missouri River

Appalachian Mountains

Death Valley
Lowest elevation in North America

Colorado River

Rio Grande

Mississippi River

Ohio River

ATLANTIC OCEAN

PACIFIC OCEAN

SIERRA MADRE OCCIDENTAL

SIERRA MADRE ORIENTAL

Gulf of Mexico

W E S T   I N D I E S

CENTRAL AMERICA

Caribbean Sea

AND PEACEFUL, GREEN VALLEYS IN THE EAST!

0 ___ 500 miles

0 ___ 750 kilometers

19

THE WEATHER REPORT

In the south, palm trees line sandy beaches. People in the Caribbean, Mexico, and Central America enjoy the sun and warmth year-round. Farther north, temperatures depend on the season. In the cool fall, some people enjoy apple picking and hiking to see the changing leaves. Winters can be cold and snowy. Spring and summer bring the heat and a chance for strong storms with tornadoes. These spinning winds are most common in the central United States. In the Caribbean and on the East Coast, major storms called hurricanes are a threat.

THE SUNNY CARIBBEAN BEACHES LOOK LIKE PARADISE.

BUT ARE YOU BIRD ENOUGH FOR A SPIN IN A TORNADO?

20

21

CRITTERS TO FIND

North America is home to a wide range of animals. In the icy north, animals built for the cold enter the scene. Polar bears hunt for seals on the sea ice. Arctic foxes dig warm burrows where they raise their pups. In the Great Plains to the south, prairie dogs and black-footed ferrets scamper in the tall grass. Bald eagles glide over forests looking for a meal. Black bears and moose lumber on the ground below. Hummingbirds slurp sweet nectar in the Central American rain forests. In the desert, rattlesnakes hunt mice and other small animals.

HELLO, MR. PRAIRIE DOG. TERENCE! DON'T MESS WITH THAT POLAR BEAR!

BALD EAGLES LOOK TOUGH! I WOULDN'T WANT TO MESS WITH THAT BIRD!

23

North America is filled with remarkable ancient wonders. The Grand Canyon amazes visitors with its size and sweeping views. The mighty Colorado River carved the canyon over billions of years. The stone pyramids at sites like Chichén Itzá and Tikal are some of the continent's oldest human-made ruins. The Maya people built them long ago.

THE GOLDEN GATE BRIDGE MATCHES MY FEATHERS!

There are plenty of modern sights to see, too. The red Golden Gate Bridge spans the place where San Francisco Bay meets the Pacific Ocean. Visitors can see the Statue of Liberty in New York Harbor. This statue has been welcoming people to the United States for more than 125 years. Baseball fans love to watch a game at the historic Fenway Park in Boston.

WE LOVE...

...LADY...

...LIBERTY!

SOUTH AMERICA

MY TURN! I'LL TAKE US THROUGH SOUTH AMERICA!

ATLAS

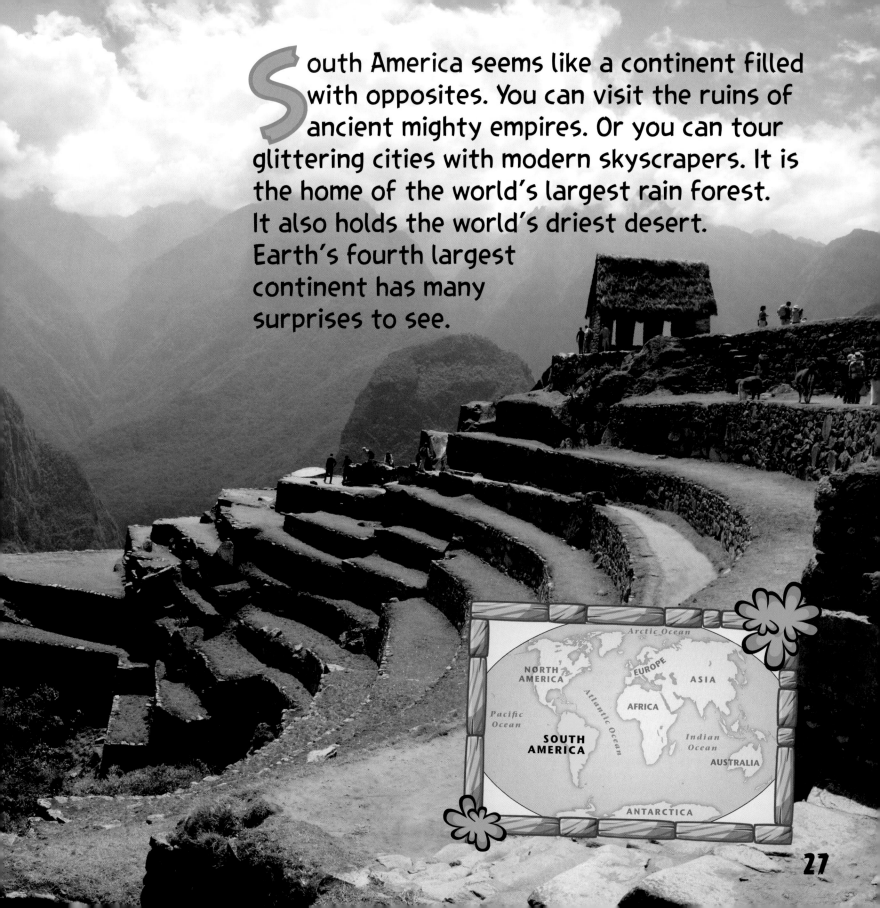

outh America seems like a continent filled with opposites. You can visit the ruins of ancient mighty empires. Or you can tour glittering cities with modern skyscrapers. It is the home of the world's largest rain forest. It also holds the world's driest desert. Earth's fourth largest continent has many surprises to see.

COUNTRIES OF SOUTH AMERICA

SOUTH AMERICA

South America is divided into 12 countries. The smallest is little Suriname. Its neighbor, French Guiana, isn't a country because it belongs to France. Brazil holds the most people and the most land within its borders. Popular foods like potatoes and tomatoes are native to South America. Today farming is a major source of business. South America's bananas, coffee, and sugar are shipped all over the world. Like sparkly green gems? Most emeralds come from mines in Colombia.

I'M CUCKOO FOR COLOMBIA!

HEY, BIRDS, WHERE IN SOUTH AMERICA DO WE WANT TO GO?

Fortaleza

Belém

Marajó Island

BRAZIL

Paramaribo

Cayenne
FRENCH GUIANA
(France)

SURINAME

Georgetown

GUYANA

Negro River

Amazon River

Manaus

Caracas

VENEZUELA

Orinoco River

Lake Maracaibo

Bogotá

COLOMBIA

Medellín

Cali

Quito

ECUADOR

Guayaquil

28

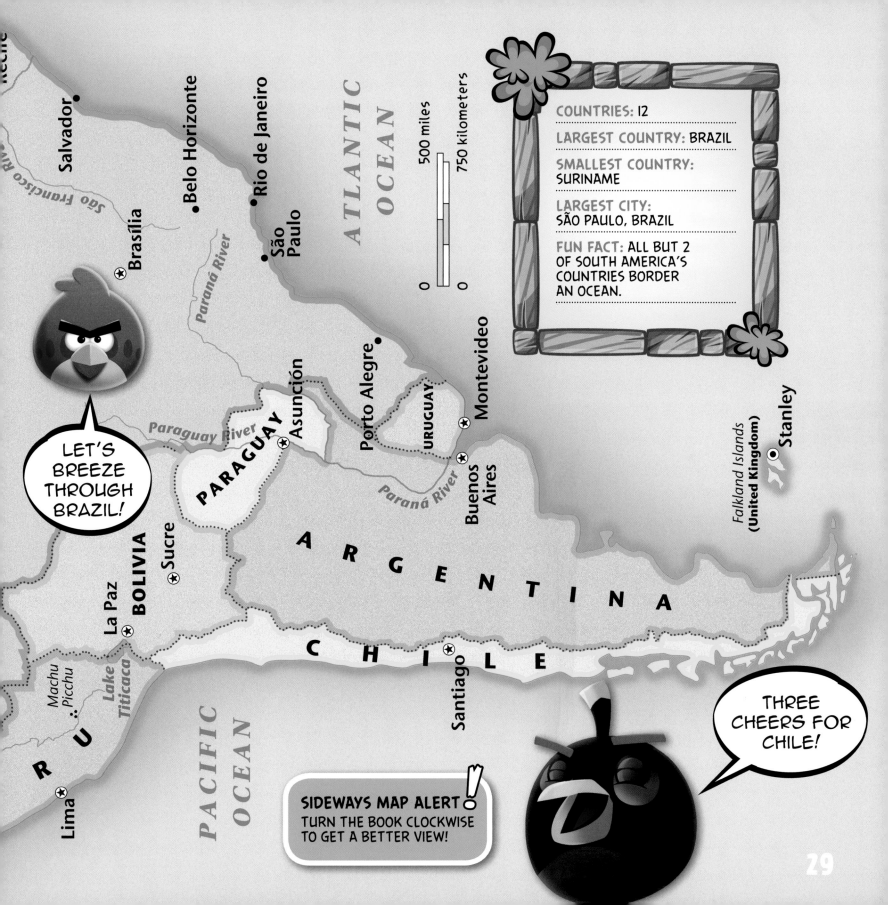

Salvador

Belo Horizonte

Rio de Janeiro

Brasília

São Paulo

São Francisco River

Paraná River

ATLANTIC OCEAN

500 miles
750 kilometers
0
0

COUNTRIES: 12
....
LARGEST COUNTRY: BRAZIL
....
SMALLEST COUNTRY:
SURINAME
....
LARGEST CITY:
SÃO PAULO, BRAZIL
....
FUN FACT: ALL BUT 2
OF SOUTH AMERICA'S
COUNTRIES BORDER
AN OCEAN.

LET'S BREEZE THROUGH BRAZIL!

Paraguay River

Asunción

PARAGUAY

Porto Alegre

URUGUAY

Montevideo

Paraná River

Buenos Aires

Stanley

Falkland Islands (United Kingdom)

Sucre

BOLIVIA

La Paz

A R G E N T I N A

C H I L E

Santiago

Machu Picchu

Lake Titicaca

PERU

Lima

PACIFIC OCEAN

SIDEWAYS MAP ALERT
TURN THE BOOK CLOCKWISE
TO GET A BETTER VIEW!

THREE CHEERS FOR CHILE!

WHO LIVES HERE?

WE'VE LEARNED ABOUT THE COUNTRIES, BUT WHAT ABOUT THE PEOPLE WHO LIVE HERE?

30

The first people to arrive in South America traveled on foot from North America. They came a very long time ago. Some civilizations, like the Inca, grew into complex empires. Their ruins can still be seen today. Colonists from Europe started to arrive about 480 years ago. They came mostly from Spain and Portugal. They brought African slaves to work in the fields. In time, the cultures started blending together. Most people in South America are related to these three groups. Spanish and Portuguese are the most common languages spoken here. Soccer is one of the most popular sports in South America. Many people look forward to the colorful celebrations of Carnival every year.

FELLOWS WITH FANCY FOOTWORK!

THEY LOOK PRETTY HAPPY TO ME!

COSTUMES AT CARNIVAL!

31

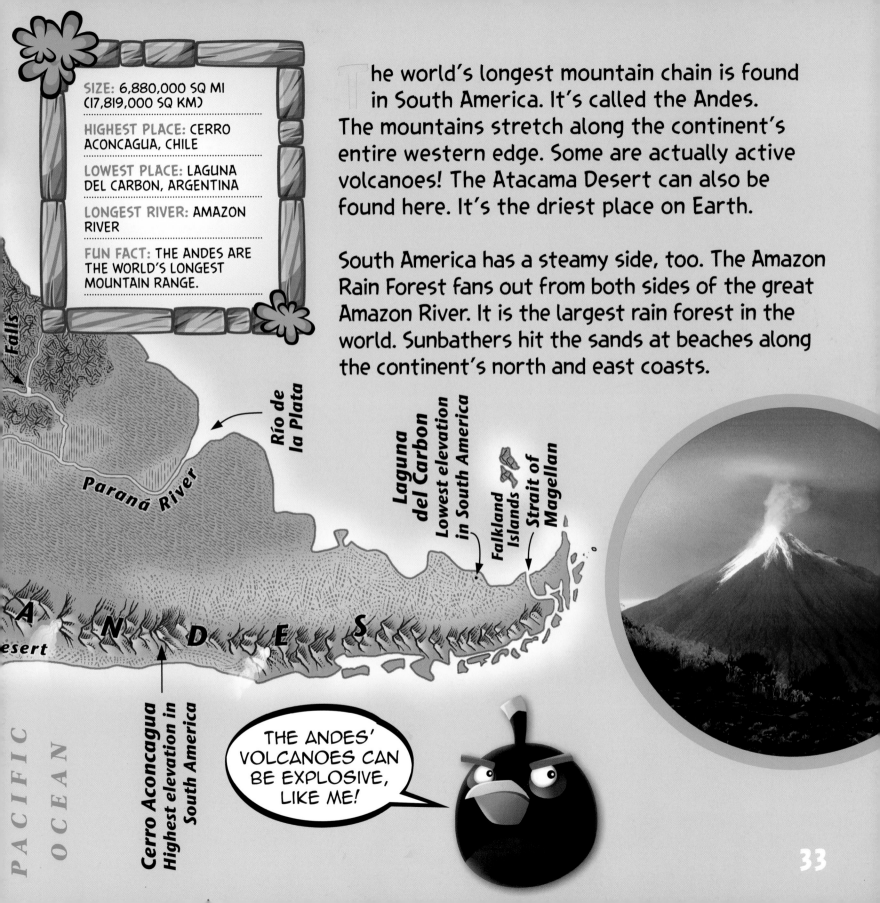

SIZE: 6,880,000 SQ MI (17,819,000 SQ KM)

HIGHEST PLACE: CERRO ACONCAGUA, CHILE

LOWEST PLACE: LAGUNA DEL CARBON, ARGENTINA

LONGEST RIVER: AMAZON RIVER

FUN FACT: THE ANDES ARE THE WORLD'S LONGEST MOUNTAIN RANGE.

The world's longest mountain chain is found in South America. It's called the Andes. The mountains stretch along the continent's entire western edge. Some are actually active volcanoes! The Atacama Desert can also be found here. It's the driest place on Earth.

South America has a steamy side, too. The Amazon Rain Forest fans out from both sides of the great Amazon River. It is the largest rain forest in the world. Sunbathers hit the sands at beaches along the continent's north and east coasts.

Falls

Río de la Plata

Paraná River

Laguna del Carbon
Lowest elevation in South America

Falkland Islands

Strait of Magellan

A N D E S

esert

Cerro Aconcagua
Highest elevation in South America

PACIFIC OCEAN

THE ANDES' VOLCANOES CAN BE EXPLOSIVE, LIKE ME!

THE WEATHER REPORT

It's often warm and sunny in the northern half of South America. Some places, like the Amazon, are hot and rainy all the time. In the north, rainy seasons bring relief from the year-round heat.

Things change in the continent's southern half. The lands are much drier in the Atacama Desert along the western coast. In many places, people have to bundle up for much of the year. It's even chillier at the tip of South America. This region is called Patagonia. Giant ice fields cover parts of the land. You can even find moving sheets of ice called glaciers.

JUST LOOKING AT THE ATACAMA DESERT IS MAKING ME THIRSTY!

35

CRITTERS TO FIND

South America is home to a very colorful group of creatures! Pink dolphins swim in a mighty river. Bright red parrots chatter in the trees. Giant green snakes can weigh as much as 550 pounds (250 kg)! The continent has a wide range of habitats, or homes, for animals. Many different types live here. Glossy seals swim in the blue waters surrounding the Galápagos Islands. Shaggy llamas can be found in mountainous Peru. Jaguars prowl the jungles of the Amazon, where a wide variety of living things can be found. A single bush can hold more species of ants than you can find in the entire United Kingdom!

LOOK AT TERENCE! HE'S COPYING THOSE RED PARROTS!

LOOK OUT! THERE ARE JAGUARS ABOUT!

37

There are many wonderful things to see in South America. Wildlife lovers flock to the Galápagos Islands. These islands off the coast of Ecuador are home to many interesting animals. Hikers might check out the parks surrounding Iguazu Falls, located between Brazil and Argentina. It's the largest series of waterfalls in the world.

A large group of ancient sculptures stands in the San Agustín Archaeological Park in Colombia. There are 500 statues of ancient gods and mythical creatures carved many centuries ago. Visitors also flock to Rio de Janeiro in Brazil to see the giant statue "Christ the Redeemer." It is almost 100 feet (30 m) tall!

AND THIS GIANT STATUE IS A WONDER OF THE WORLD!

THE ANIMALS IN THE GALÁPAGOS ISLANDS ARE WONDERFUL, TOO!

EUROPE

NOW IT'S MY TURN! I CHOOSE EUROPE. I WONDER WHAT WE'LL FIND THERE.

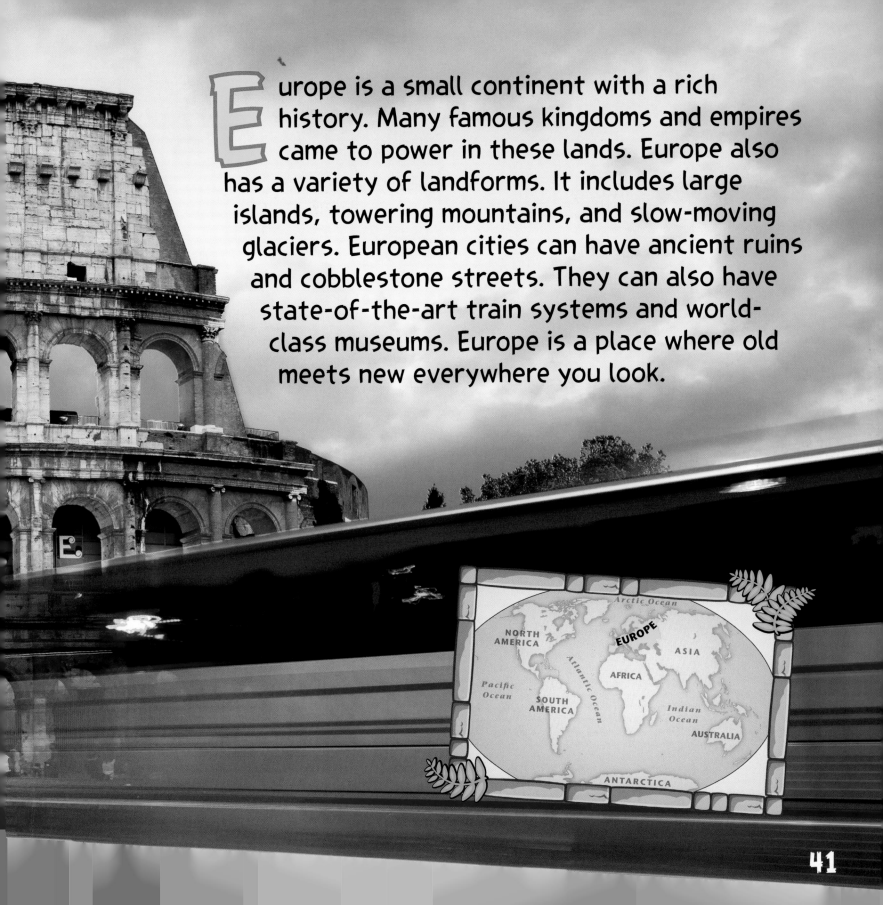

Europe is a small continent with a rich history. Many famous kingdoms and empires came to power in these lands. Europe also has a variety of landforms. It includes large islands, towering mountains, and slow-moving glaciers. European cities can have ancient ruins and cobblestone streets. They can also have state-of-the-art train systems and world-class museums. Europe is a place where old meets new everywhere you look.

COUNTRIES OF EUROPE

Europe contains 46 countries. Russia is the largest. Most of Russia's land is in Asia. Since Russia's major cities are in Europe, though, it's considered a European country. Most of Europe's major cities are located on rivers or near the ocean. London, in the United Kingdom, is the continent's largest city. Europe is a major producer of cars and machinery. Wheat, fruit, and olives grown in the south are an important part of Europe's economy.

THE UNITED KINGDOM SOUNDS JOLLY GOOD!

EUROPE HAS SO MANY COUNTRIES TO CHOOSE FROM! WHERE SHOULD WE GO NOW?

ICELAND
★ Reykjavík

Faroe Islands
(Denmark)

ATLANTIC OCEAN

Orkney Islands

Edinburgh •

IRELAND   UNITED
Dublin ★
                KINGDOM

London ★

English Channel

Paris

FRANCE

• Bordeaux

PORTUGAL
Lisbon ★
                        ANDORRA
                ★ Madrid

SPAIN

• Seville

Balearic Islands

GIBRALTAR
(U.K.)

0   500 miles

0   750 kilometers

Europe may be small, but its people are of many cultures. Each country often has its own language, customs, and food. Many Europeans speak more than one language. Over time, vast empires have come and gone here. Greek, Roman, and Ottoman people controlled large parts of the continent. Their rule had a lasting impact on the art and culture of the region. Today most Europeans are very proud of their country's unique heritage.

I WANT TO GO DANCING IN LATVIA!

HEY, LOOK! A PARADE IN IRELAND.

I WONDER IF I'D BE ANY GOOD AT HERDING SHEEP IN ICELAND...

LAY OF THE LAND

On a map, Europe and Asia look like one big continent. But they're separated by Russia's Ural Mountains. The Caucasus Mountains and Caspian Sea form the border in the southeast. Skiers delight in hitting the slopes of the Alps. Much of Europe is flat, and crops, like lavender, are grown here.

The continent has many large rivers. They've served as trade routes for centuries. Goods like grain, wool, and timber were moved along these waterways. The Volga is the longest river in Europe.

MMMMMM! FRENCH LAVENDER SMELLS HEAVENLY!

Iceland

ATLANTIC OCEAN

Ireland

PYRENEES

IBERIAN PENINSULA

BRRRRRR! THE SNOWY ALPS ARE COLD!

46

| 0 | 500 miles |
| 0 | 750 kilometer |

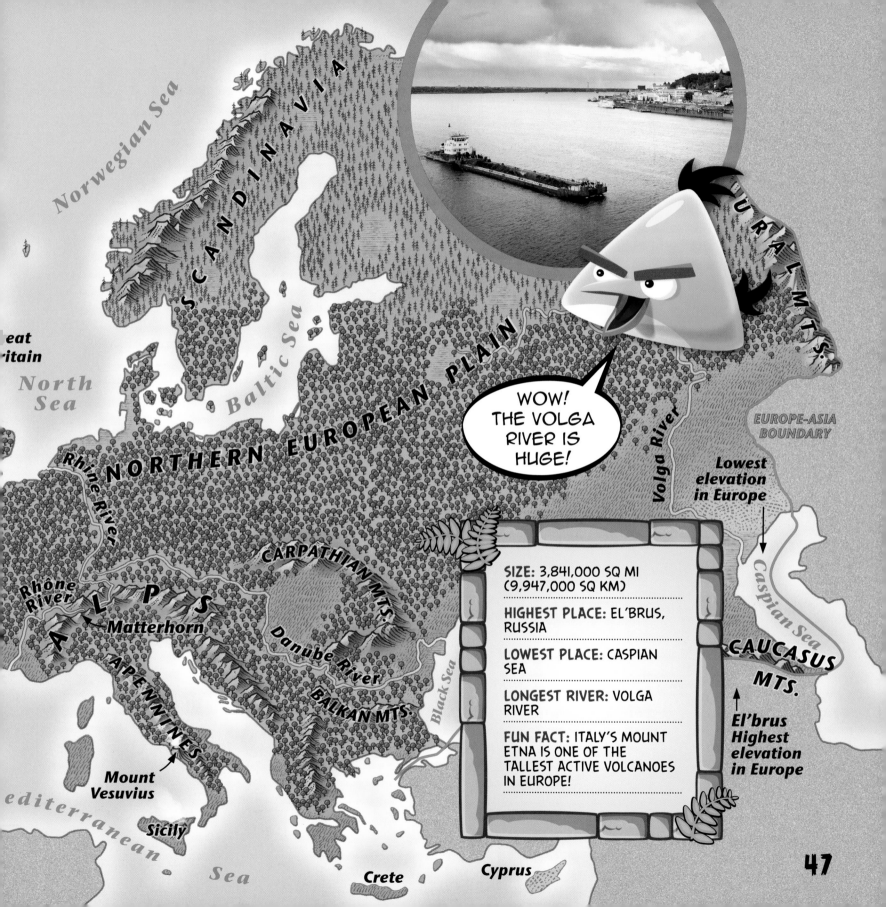

SCANDINAVIA

Norwegian Sea

Baltic Sea

North Sea

eat ritain

URAL MTS.

NORTHERN EUROPEAN PLAIN

WOW! THE VOLGA RIVER IS HUGE!

Volga River

EUROPE-ASIA BOUNDARY

Lowest elevation in Europe

Rhine River

Rhône River

ALPS

Matterhorn

CARPATHIAN MTS.

Danube River

BALKAN MTS.

Black Sea

Caspian Sea

CAUCASUS MTS.

El'brus Highest elevation in Europe

APENNINES

Mount Vesuvius

SIZE: 3,841,000 SQ MI (9,947,000 SQ KM)

HIGHEST PLACE: EL'BRUS, RUSSIA

LOWEST PLACE: CASPIAN SEA

LONGEST RIVER: VOLGA RIVER

FUN FACT: ITALY'S MOUNT ETNA IS ONE OF THE TALLEST ACTIVE VOLCANOES IN EUROPE!

Mediterranean Sea

Sicily

Crete

Cyprus

THE WEATHER REPORT

EUROPE

Europe has a mild climate. Much of the land is good for farming. In western Europe, warm ocean air keeps the winters from getting too cold. It frequently rains, especially in the British Isles. This isn't the case for eastern and central Europe. In places like Germany's Black Forest, winters are usually quite frosty. In the south, countries along the Mediterranean Sea enjoy beach weather year-round.

THE SEASONS IN EUROPE ARE SO COLORFUL!

IF I HID IN HOLLAND'S SPRING TULIPS, I'D NEVER BE FOUND!

49

CRITTERS TO FIND

Europe's woodlands provide a home for many animals. Rabbits, red squirrels, and otters live throughout the continent. Owls soar through the night sky, snapping up their prey. In the far north, reindeer roam the frozen plains. People known as the Sami live side by side with some of the great herds. In the Alps, goats called ibex balance on steep mountain cliffs. Males sometimes fight each other with the long, curved horns on their heads.

HANG ON, I'M HAVING A STARING CONTEST WITH THESE IBEX.

MAYBE WE "OTTER" ASK THIS CRITTER ABOUT EUROPE?

THIS FUNNY RED SQUIRREL HAS HAIR THAT STICKS UP LIKE MY FEATHERS!

PLACES TO SEE

EUROPE

STONEHENGE!

EVEN TERENCE...

...COULD HIDE HERE!

CHECK OUT THIS STORYBOOK CASTLE IN ROMANIA!

Europe has no shortage of cool sights. Ancient ruins like Stonehenge and the Parthenon attract history buffs. People who lived thousands of years ago made these structures. In medieval times, Europeans built castles and fortresses, such as Bran Castle in Romania. The Prague Astronomical Clock was built in 1410 and still works today! There are many younger landmarks, too. The Eiffel Tower was completed in the last 125 years.

People looking for outdoor adventures also have options. Hikers love to explore the tall mountains of the Alps, including the Matterhorn and Mont Blanc. The White Cliffs of Dover look like walls of chalk rising out of the sea. The cliffs still greet visitors sailing to England.

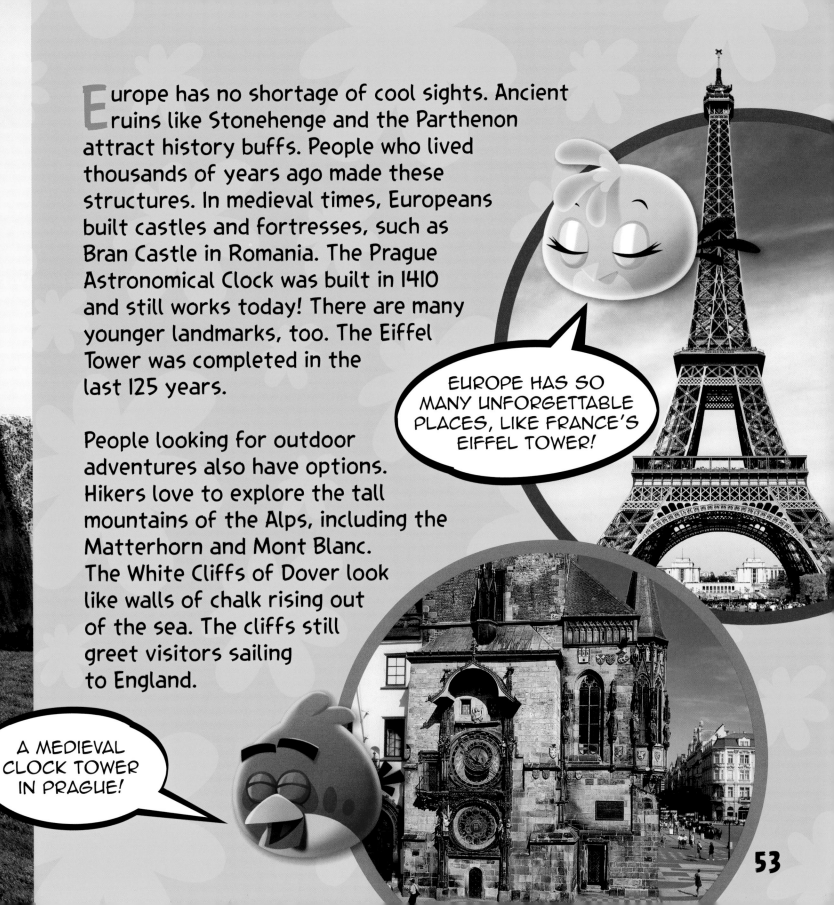

EUROPE HAS SO MANY UNFORGETTABLE PLACES, LIKE FRANCE'S EIFFEL TOWER!

A MEDIEVAL CLOCK TOWER IN PRAGUE!

53

Africa is a place that thinks big! Jumbo elephants stomp over wide grassy plains. Huge crocodiles swim through the Nile. That's the world's longest river. Round hippos wade in flooded marshes. The world's largest hot desert, the Sahara, is here. Big cities like Nairobi and Johannesburg are, too. Earth's second largest continent has lots of exciting things to see!

COUNTRIES OF AFRICA

Africa is divided into 54 countries. The newest, South Sudan, recently formed in 2011. Algeria has the most land. Nigeria has the most people. Lagos in Nigeria is the largest city in Africa. But most people on the continent live in smaller villages and farms rather than in cities.

Like chocolate? Much of the world's cocoa beans come from Africa. They're used to make chocolate treats. Mining for gold, diamonds, and minerals is also big business here.

TERENCE LOOKS LIKE HE'S HEADED TO EGYPT. WHERE SHOULD THE REST OF US GO?

SIDEWAYS MAP ALERT!
TURN THE BOOK CLOCKWISE TO GET A BETTER VIEW!

600 miles

0

Mediterranean Sea

Alexandria

Tripoli

Tunis ⊛ TUNISIA

⊛ Algiers

Rabat ⊛

Casablanca ● MOROCCO

Canary Islands

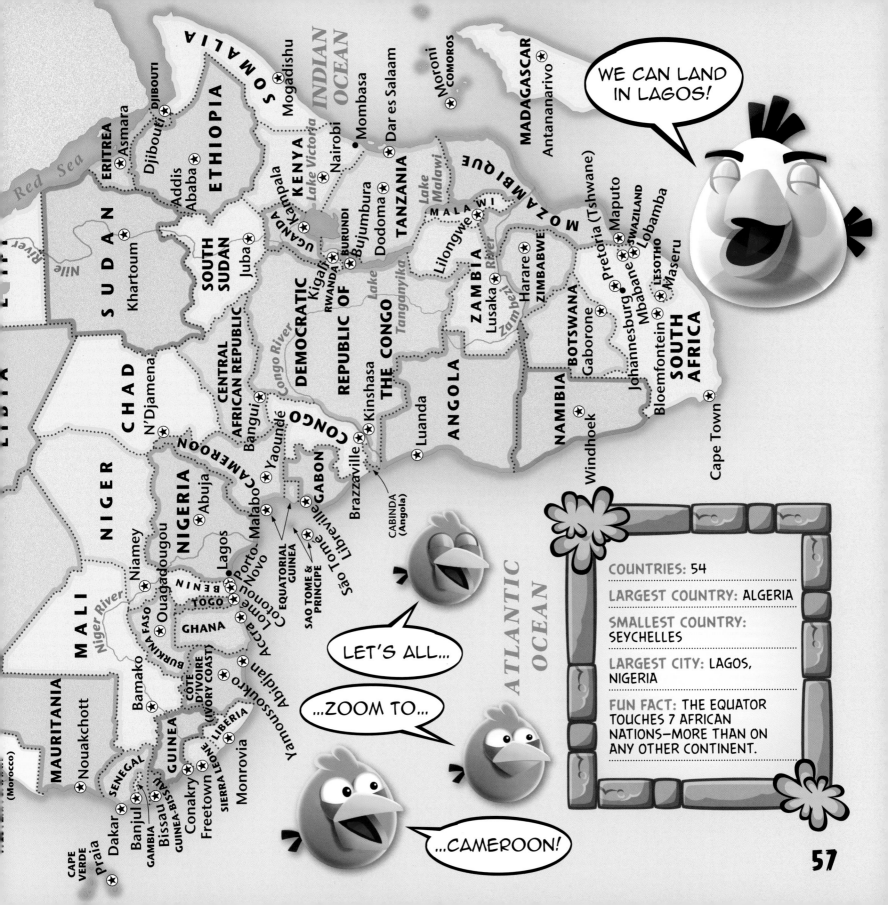

People have lived in Africa longer than any other place in the world. Scientists believe that human beginnings can be traced here. Fossils of our earliest ancestors have been found on this continent.

Today many different peoples call Africa home. North African countries like Morocco and Egypt have much in common with nearby Middle Eastern nations.

The lands south of the Sahara desert contain hundreds of cultures, many with their own languages. Many people live in huge modern cities, like Lagos in Nigeria. Other groups favor their traditional ways of life, like the nomadic Maasai of eastern Africa.

People of European descent also live here. Many of Africa's countries were ruled by European nations from the 17th to the 20th century. Most countries became independent by the end of the 1960s.

THESE GUYS LOOK LIKE THEY'RE HAVING FUN!

WHAT COLORFUL CLOTHES!

LAY OF THE LAND

AFRICA

A huge desert, the Sahara, covers the entire northern part of the continent. A band of rain forests lies across the middle. Grasslands called savanna cover the rest of the continent. The long Nile River winds from the center of Africa to the Mediterranean Sea in the north.

Small mountain ranges can be found in Africa. Most are in the Great Rift Valley. Many of Africa's largest lakes are located here, too.

...STRETCHES FROM HERE...

THE GREAT BIG NILE...

THE GREAT RIFT VALLEY COVERS MUCH OF WESTERN AFRICA!

ATLAS MOUNTAINS

SIDEWAYS MAP ALERT! TURN THE BOOK CLOCKWISE TO GET A BETTER VIEW!

60

THE WEATHER REPORT

Most places in Africa are hot. Oven-like heat happens every day in areas in and around the Sahara. It's always warm and wet in the continent's rain forests. Most of the grasslands have wet and dry seasons. The animals here often cover great distances with these seasons. They're looking for food and water.

It's rarely very cold in Africa. The chilliest spots are on top of the few mountains, such as Mount Kilimanjaro in Tanzania.

HOT AND HUMID RAIN FORESTS!

AFRICA IS HOT! TERENCE, ANY LUCK COOLING OFF UNDER THAT TREE?

CRITTERS TO FIND

You've probably heard of some of the animals that live in Africa. Lions, giraffes, and elephants are just some of the famous creatures that live here. They're found mainly in the grasslands. Chimps hang out in the woodlands. Stinging scorpions crawl over the desert sands. Lemurs rule the rain forests in Madagascar, Africa's largest island. You'll even find penguins at the tip of South Africa!

I CAN'T LOOK. TELL ME WHEN THE SCORPION'S GONE.

WHAT A COUPLE OF LOVEBIRDS!

65

PLACES TO SEE

AFRICA

THE GREAT SPHINX IS AS SILENT AS TERENCE!

I WONDER WHAT WE'D SEE ON A SAFARI IN THE OKAVANGO DELTA...

66

Every year, visitors take in sights like Egypt's Great Sphinx and mighty pyramids. Ancient Egyptians built them more than 4,500 years ago. In Morocco, shoppers stroll through colorful markets called souks. Vendors sell goods like spices, rugs, silk, and jewelry.

Others might go on a safari to the Okavango Delta in Botswana. Much of the area is protected by national parks and reserves. Farther north, people can hike through the Virunga Mountains in hopes of spotting a mountain gorilla.

WE NEED TO GO TO THE MOUNTAINS TO FIND GORILLAS...

...AND TO MOROCCO TO BUY SPICES. YUM!

67

Asia is the world's largest continent. Earth's highest point, the top of Mount Everest, is here. So is the lowest—the shore of the salty Dead Sea. More people live in Asia than anywhere else. The world's first cities were built in its green river valleys. The continent is even home to the largest structure ever built by humans: the Great Wall of China.

COUNTRIES OF ASIA

Asia has 46 countries. Russia takes up a large part of the land, but it's counted as part of Europe (see pages 42–43). China is the largest country that fits completely within Asia's borders. Many of the world's most crowded cities are here. Tokyo in Japan has the most people. More than 32 million call it home.

Many people in Asia make a living from the land. Farming, especially growing rice, is very important. Nearly all of the world's supply of rice comes from Asia.

COUNTRIES: 46

LARGEST COUNTRY:
PEOPLE'S REPUBLIC OF CHINA

SMALLEST COUNTRY:
MALDIVES

LARGEST CITY: TOKYO,
JAPAN

FUN FACT: CHINA SHARES
ITS BORDERS WITH 14
OTHER COUNTRIES.

Istanbul
Ankara ⊛ TURK
LEBANON
Beirut ⊛
Damascus ⊛ SYR
Jerusalem ⊛ ⊛
ISRAEL ⊛ Amm
JORDAN IRA
Baghd
KUW
Kuw
SAUD
Riyadh ⊛
ARAB
⊛ Sanaa
YEME

Red Sea

HEY, BIRDS!
THE BOOK SAYS
ASIA IS THE
WORLD'S BIGGEST
CONTINENT.

IT HAS SOME
PRETTY SMALL
COUNTRIES...

71

More people live in Asia than anywhere else. It's home to people of many different cultures. These cultures have their own language and traditions. Sometimes even neighbors have trouble understanding each other. The Chinese language, for example, has many dialects. People from one city may not understand the type of Chinese spoken in another.

People in Asia have fun in many different ways. In India, many children enjoy playing cricket. All over the continent, holidays and festivals bring families together to celebrate. Red paper lanterns are a popular sight during Chinese New Year. Each region has its own way of cooking food, too. Many of these dishes are popular around the world.

CRICKET IS CRACKING IN INDIA!

STROLLING UNDER PRETTY LANTERNS IN CHINA!

LAY OF THE LAND

ASIA

Much of the land in Asia is a harsh place to live. It's either too high, too dry, or too cold to support cities. The world's highest mountains, the Himalaya, lie across the south. Great sandy deserts stretch across southwestern and central Asia. The Gobi, in central Asia, is sometimes called the Endless Sea. It's like a sea of sand.

So where do all of Asia's people live? Most cities and villages are along the coast or on rivers. Some areas in the southeast are very green and lush. They're great for farming.

THE TOP OF MOUNT EVEREST LOOKS BLUE AND WHITE.

THE GOBI'S DESERT SANDS ARE GOLDEN.

ARCTI

EUROPE-ASIA BOUNDARY

Black Sea

CAUCASUS MTS.

Caspian Sea

Tr

Dead Sea
Lowest elevation in Asia

Persian Gulf

ARABIAN PENINSULA

Ind

Arabian Sea

INDIAN OCEAN

| 0 | 600 miles |
| 0 | 900 kilometers |

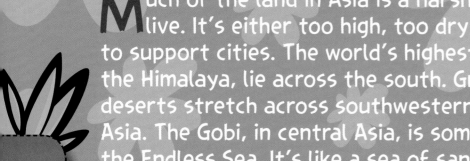

THE WEATHER REPORT

You can experience a huge range of climates in Asia. In the north, winters are long and very cold. Some of the land is frozen year-round. Huge, dry deserts can be either very hot or a mix of hot and cold. In the Gobi desert, the temperature can change by 95°F (35°C) in a single day! Rain forests grow in southeast Asia, where it is warm and damp. Rains called monsoons drench parts of India and southern Asia every summer. These rains are important for refilling water supplies and growing crops.

ASIA'S WEATHER HAS SO MUCH VARIETY. THE DESERT IS DRY.

CRITTERS TO FIND

Asia is home to many animals found nowhere else. Giant pandas live only in the bamboo forests of southwestern China. Orangutans are found in the rain forests of the islands Sumatra and Borneo. You'll find Komodo dragons only in Indonesia. At more than 300 pounds (136 kg), they're the world's biggest lizards. Tigers once roamed widely across Asia. Today they are only found in small numbers in southeast Asia and eastern Russia. The flashy peacock also lives in southeast Asia. It's the national bird of India.

THERE ARE SO MANY COOL CRITTERS YOU CAN ONLY FIND IN ASIA!

THIS PANDA IS SO PRECIOUS!

KOMODO DRAGONS ARE HUGE! I'M GLAD I WON'T RUN INTO HIM ON PIGGY ISLAND!

ASIA HAS SO MANY PLACES—NEW AND OLD— TO EXPLORE!

Asia has many beautiful buildings and temples. Some are holy sites, like the Hindu temples of Angkor Wat. You can also find the ruins of ancient cities. Petra was carved from rock more than 2,000 years ago.

Asia's natural wonders are breathtaking, too! The Classical Gardens in Suzhou, China, are more than a thousand years old. Visitors can see traditional buildings called pagodas among the flowers and trees. The sparkling blue waters off the coast of Thailand attract many visitors who come for the beaches.

THAILAND'S BLUE WATERS ARE BEAUTIFUL!

WOW! A PETRIFIED PALACE!

AUSTRALIA

HOORAY! IT'S MY TURN. LET'S FIND OUT ABOUT AUSTRALIA!

ATLAS

Australia is the only continent that's also its own country. Australians call it the "Land Down Under." That's because the whole continent lies south of, or under, the Equator. This imaginary line divides the world into a north half and a south half. Australia's neighbors include the country of New Zealand and the islands of Oceania. Australia is the world's smallest continent. But it has many unusual and beautiful features.

COUNTRY OF AUSTRALIA

Australia is divided into six states and two territories. The continent's closest neighbors are islands like New Zealand and other nations in the South Pacific Ocean. The middle part of the country is a hot, rocky desert. It's known as the Outback. Very few people live there. Most Australians live in cities near the coasts. Sydney is the largest city. Canberra is the capital.

Sheep and cattle ranching is a major source of business in Australia. The country is the world's largest wool producer. In fact, sheep outnumber people 7 to 1!

WELCOME TO AUSTRALIA, BIRDS! WHERE SHOULD WE LOOK FIRST?

Port Hedland

WESTERI

Perth

DO YOU COME FROM "THE LAND DOWN UNDER"?

WHO LIVES HERE?

P eople first reached Australia more than 40,000 years ago. This group, called Aborigines, came from Asia. Today, most Aborigines live in the Northern Territory. More than 250 languages are spoken among them.

Europeans began arriving on the continent in the 1700s. They were mainly from England. Most Australians are related to these settlers. In recent years, immigrants from all over the world have come to Australia. But English is still the main language.

CELEBRATING TIMELESS TRADITIONS!

IT LOOKS LIKE AUSSIES LOVE TO GET OUTSIDE AND GO!

G'DAY MATES! GOOD DAY TO GO RAFTING?

LAY OF THE LAND

AUSTRALIA

Along mountain range runs down the eastern side of Australia. It's called the Great Dividing Range. The Australian Alps lie in the south. They include Mount Kosciuszko, the country's tallest peak.

The rest of the continent is mainly flat. It's covered by either grasslands or deserts. The Murray and Darling Rivers make up the continent's largest river system. It provides much-needed water to Australia's farmlands in the southeast.

TALL GRASSES IN THE VALLEYS!

Hamersley Range

Darling Range

LUSH GREEN PLANTS BY THE RIVERS!

INDIAN OCEAN

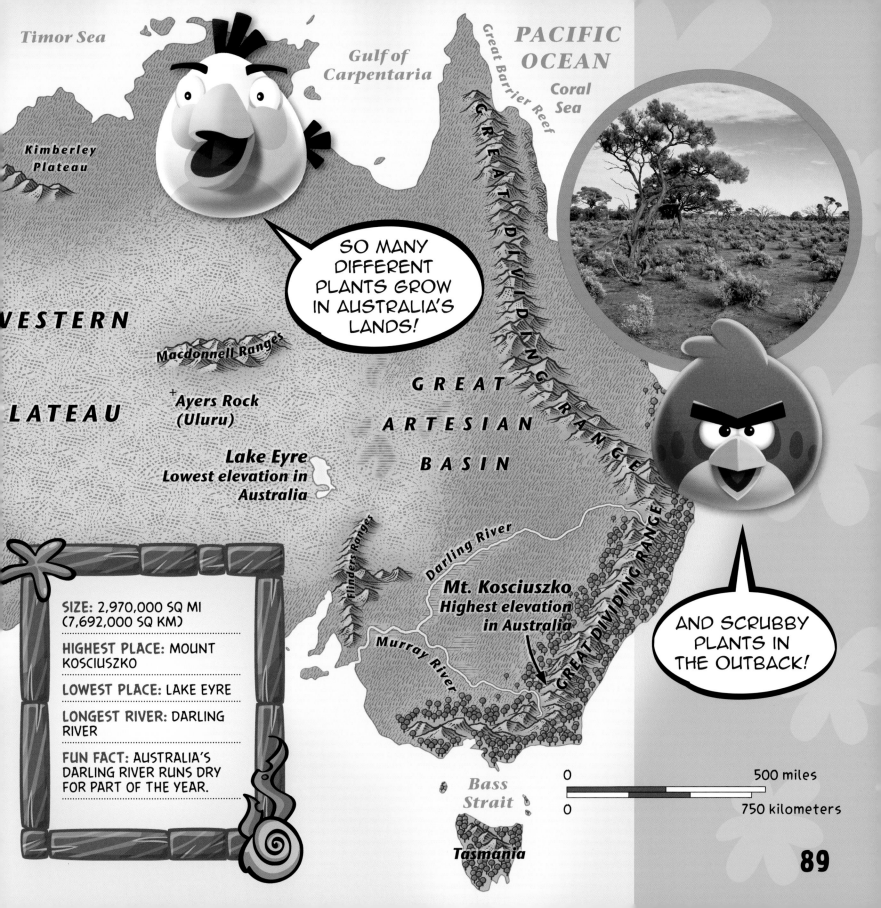

Timor Sea

Gulf of Carpentaria

PACIFIC OCEAN

Coral Sea

Great Barrier Reef

GREAT DIVIDING RANGE

Kimberley Plateau

SO MANY DIFFERENT PLANTS GROW IN AUSTRALIA'S LANDS!

WESTERN

PLATEAU

Macdonnell Ranges

+Ayers Rock (Uluru)

GREAT ARTESIAN BASIN

Lake Eyre
Lowest elevation in Australia

Flinders Ranges

Darling River

Mt. Kosciuszko
Highest elevation in Australia

Murray River

GREAT DIVIDING RANGE

AND SCRUBBY PLANTS IN THE OUTBACK!

SIZE: 2,970,000 SQ MI (7,692,000 SQ KM)

HIGHEST PLACE: MOUNT KOSCIUSZKO

LOWEST PLACE: LAKE EYRE

LONGEST RIVER: DARLING RIVER

FUN FACT: AUSTRALIA'S DARLING RIVER RUNS DRY FOR PART OF THE YEAR.

Bass Strait

0   500 miles
0   750 kilometers

Tasmania

89

THE WEATHER REPORT

Most of Australia is warm year-round. The center and west side of the continent are usually dry. Seasonal winds bring rain to the northern coast. This allows forests to grow here.

During the Australian summer, cyclones are a major threat. These swirling storms are just like hurricanes, except they spin in the opposite direction. Cyclone season happens between November and the end of April every year.

CYCLONES ARE ENORMOUS!

THESE PLATEAUS LOOK DUSTY.

90

CRITTERS TO FIND

Earth's largest living structure lies off Australia's northeast coast. The Great Barrier Reef is so big, it can be seen from space! It stretches 1,250 miles (2,012 km) through the Coral Sea.

Back on land, Australia hosts many unusual animals. Animals like kangaroos and koalas raise their young in pouches on their bellies. The hefty emu is Australia's largest bird. It can't fly. It uses powerful legs for running and kicking. The titan stick insect tries to blend in on trees in Australia's eastern forests.

A BUG THAT LOOKS LIKE A STICK?!?

KANGAROO MOMS HAVE BUILT-IN CAR SEATS!

92

93

PLACES TO SEE

ULURU? THAT'S A GREAT WORD!

TAKE A LOOK AT THOSE STEAMY HOT SPRINGS!

Australia and New Zealand are filled with fascinating sights. In New Zealand, visitors flock to see the steamy waters of Rotorua Hot Springs.

In Australia, an ancient rock mound called Uluru is a popular natural landmark. Its English name is Ayers Rock. The site is very special to some Aborigines. Rock caves covered in ancient paintings surround the area. Uluru looks like it's glowing red at sunrise and sunset. The busy city of Sydney is a great place to shop or see a show. The famous Sydney Opera House overlooks one of the world's largest natural harbors.

FA

LA

LA LA LA!

THESE PLACES ARE AWESOME!

ANTARCTICA

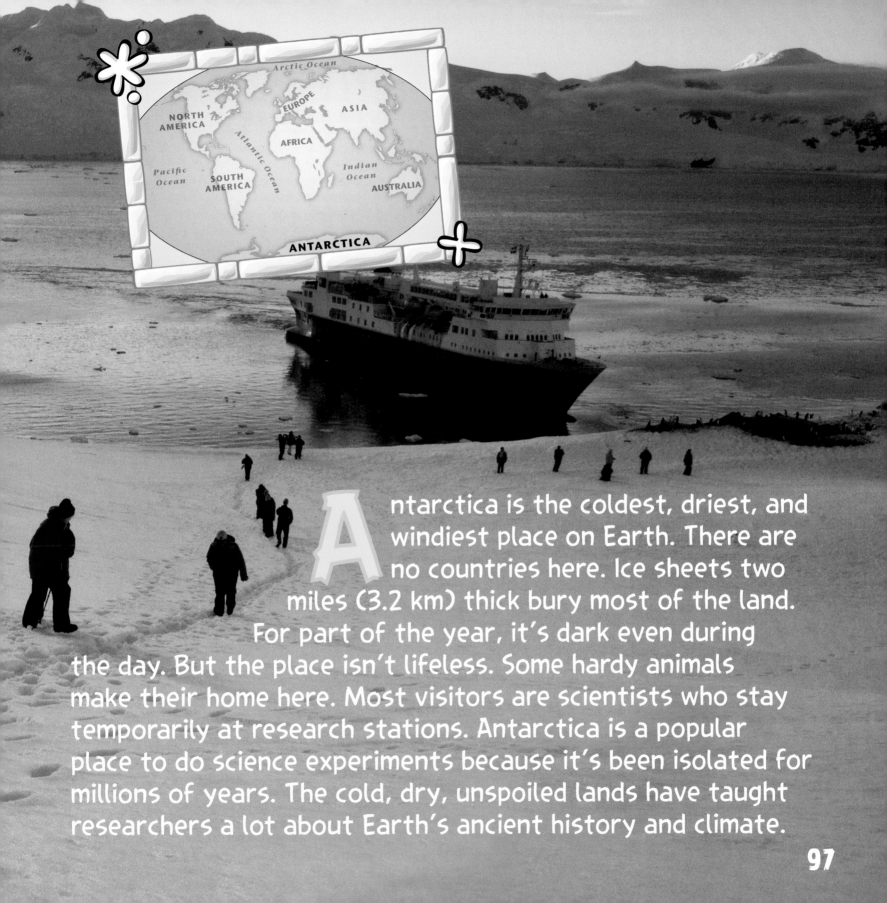

Antarctica is the coldest, driest, and windiest place on Earth. There are no countries here. Ice sheets two miles (3.2 km) thick bury most of the land. For part of the year, it's dark even during the day. But the place isn't lifeless. Some hardy animals make their home here. Most visitors are scientists who stay temporarily at research stations. Antarctica is a popular place to do science experiments because it's been isolated for millions of years. The cold, dry, unspoiled lands have taught researchers a lot about Earth's ancient history and climate.

LAY OF THE LAND

Antarctica is the landmass that covers the South Pole. It is the fifth largest continent. It's larger than Europe, but smaller than South America.

A long mountain range divides Antarctica into two sides. East Antarctica is mostly high, flat plain that's covered in ice. Mountains stretch across West Antarctica. The continent's highest peak, Vinson Massif, is found in the west. Mount Sidley, a towering, ice-covered volcano, is located there too.

ANTARCTICA

THE ICE GOES ON FOREVER!

VINSON MASSIF IS ONE TALL MOUNTAIN!

ANTARCTIC PENINSULA

ELLSWORT

LAN

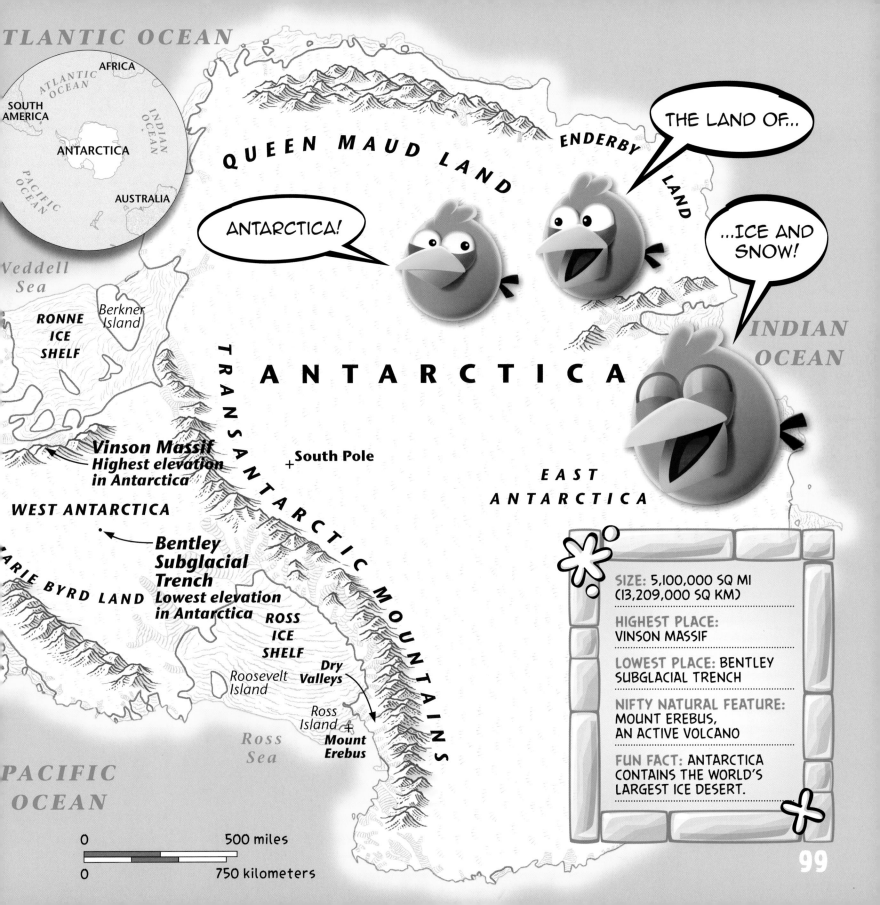

THE WEATHER REPORT

The weather in Antarctica is easy to predict. It's always cold! Temperatures rarely rise above freezing. Once a thermometer at a research station here read –128.6°F (–89.2°C). That's the lowest temperature ever recorded on Earth! One of the few places where things warm up is on Mount Erebus, the most active volcano on the continent.

Antarctica gets very little rain or snow. Most of the time, only two inches of snow falls per year. The dry conditions make Antarctica one big desert. The thick ice cap that covers the land took millions of years to build up.

RESEARCHERS STAY IN THESE TENTS!

HOW CAN WE STAY WARM WITH ALL THIS ICE AND SNOW?

101

CRITTERS TO FIND

It's tough to survive on the land in Antarctica. But the waters around the continent are rich in food and nutrients. Many animals come here to feed in the oceans. Seabirds nest along the coast during the short Antarctic summer. Blue whales and humpback whales travel here to feed on krill. Krill are tiny shrimp-like animals. Emperor penguins are one of the few animals to stay in Antarctica year-round. They huddle together to keep warm during the freezing winter months.

ANTARCTICA'S FROSTY WEATHER IS NO PROBLEM FOR THESE ANIMALS!

I'D LOVE TO SEE A WHALE. WOULDN'T YOU, TERENCE?

102

STOP FIGHTING, YOU GUYS! WE CAN ALL LOOK.

STOP. STOP! STOP!

BLAM

SETTLE DOWN, BOMB. I HAVE AN IDEA. WE'VE LEARNED SO MUCH ABOUT THE WORLD, WHY DON'T WE MAKE OUR OWN ATLAS OF PIGGY ISLAND?

I'LL GET THE PAPER!

WE'LL GET THE PENCILS!

I'LL GET THE CAMERA!

THAT'S A GREAT IDEA!

LET'S GET STARTED!

So the birds took everything they learned and started their very own Atlas of Piggy Island.

Where do you think Piggy Island can be found?

105

WORLD MAP

Use this world map to find each of the continents where these amazing sights and creatures can be found.

NORTH AMERICA
Rocky Mountains
Prairie dogs
Grand Canyon
Statue of Liberty

EUROPE
The Alps
Ibex
Bran Castle
Eiffel Tower

SOUTH AMERICA
Amazon River
Jaguars
Iguazu Falls
Machu Picchu

ROCKY MTS.

GREAT PLAINS

NORTH AMERICA

GRAND CANYON
U.S.A.

STATUE OF LIBERTY
New York, U.S.A.

PACIFIC
OCEAN

EQUATOR

Amazon River

MACHU PICCHU
Peru

**SOUTH
AMERICA**

IGUAZU FALLS
Brazil/Argentina

ATLANTIC
OCEAN

VINSON MASSIF

ARCTIC OCEAN

EIFFEL TOWER
Paris, France

EUROPE

ALPS

BRAN CASTLE
Romania

PYRAMIDS AT GIZA
Egypt

PETRA
Jordan

SAHARA

AFRICA

Nile River

A
S
I
A

MOUNT EVEREST
China/Nepal

GOBI

ASIA
Gobi
Giant pandas
Mount Everest
Petra

PACIFIC
OCEAN

AFRICA
Sahara
Lemurs
Nile River
Great Pyramids

EQUATOR

INDIAN
OCEAN

Great
Barrier
Reef

AUSTRALIA

ULURU (AYERS ROCK)

OPERA HOUSE
Sydney

AUSTRALIA
Great Barrier Reef
Kangaroos
Uluru (Ayers Rock)
Sydney Opera House

ANTARCTICA
Vinson Massif
Emperor penguins
Mount Erebus

MOUNT EREBUS

ANTARCTICA

0   2,000 miles

0   3,000 kilometers

107

QUIZ TIME!

1. Which is the only continent that does not have the letter "**A**" in its name?

2. This is a picture of the Nile. The Nile is the world's longest _____.

    a. river
    b. ocean
    c. street
    d. tunnel
    e. None of the above

3. The pigs have stolen some of the letters from the names of the world's four oceans. Can you figure out what letters are missing?

    a. ___ACIFIC OCEAN
    b. ATLA___TIC OCEAN
    c. IN___IAN OCEAN
    d. AR___TIC OCEAN

4. Match these animals with the continents where they live in the wild:

1. Lion
2. Bald eagle
3. Giant panda
4. Koala

a. Asia
b. Africa
c. Australia
d. North America

5. Geography True or False

See if you can tell which sentences are true and which ones are false.

a. The world's highest point is found in Asia.
b. The Alps are the mountains that separate Europe from Asia.
c. The Grand Canyon is located in Australia.
d. The Sahara desert covers much of northern Africa.

1. Europe   2. a. river   3. a, P, N, c, D, d, c   4. 1-b, 2-d, 3-a, 4-c   5. a: True, b: False (The Urals separate Europe from Asia), c: False (The Grand Canyon is in North America), d: True

109

BONUS MATERIAL

LAND
The continents, from largest to smallest

1. Asia: 17,208,000 sq mi (44,570,000 sq km)
2. Africa: 11,608,000 sq mi (30,065,000 sq km)
3. North America: 9,499,000 sq mi (24,474,000 sq km)
4. South America: 6,880,000 sq mi (17,819,000 sq km)
5. Antarctica: 5,100,000 sq mi (13,209,000 sq km)
6. Europe: 3,841,000 sq mi (9,947,000 sq km)
7. Australia: 2,970,000 sq mi (7,692,000 sq km)

OCEANS
The world's oceans, from largest to smallest

1. Pacific Ocean: 65,436,200 sq mi (169,479,000 sq km)
2. Atlantic Ocean: 35,338,500 sq mi (91,526,400 sq km)
3. Indian Ocean: 28,839,800 sq mi (74,694,700 sq km)
4. Arctic Ocean: 5,390,000 sq mi (13,960,100 sq km)

WORLD RECORD HOLDERS
Here's a list of the world's largest, tallest, and longest places.

World's Tallest Mountain (on land)
Mount Everest, located in Asia
29,035 ft (8,850 m) tall

World's Lowest Point (on land)
Dead Sea, located in Asia
-1,385 ft (-422 m)

World's Largest Island
Greenland, found in the Arctic
and Atlantic Oceans
836,000 sq mi (2,166,000 sq km)

World's Longest River
Nile River, in Africa
4,400 mi (7,081 km)

World's Largest Freshwater Lake
Lake Superior, in North America
31,700 sq mi (82,100 sq km)

World's Largest Saltwater Lake
Caspian Sea, located between
Europe and Asia
143,000 sq mi (371,000 sq km)

World's Longest Mountain Range (on land)
Andes, in South America
4,500 mi (7,200 km)

World's Coldest Place
Vostok Research Station, found
in Antarctica
-128.6°F (-89.2°C)
recorded 1983

World's Hottest Place
Death Valley, found in North America
134°F (56.7°C)
recorded 1913

World's Most Populous Country
China, in Asia
1,331,398,000 people

World's Largest Country
Russia, in Europe and Asia
6,592,850 sq mi (17,075,400 sq km)

World's Smallest Country
Vatican City, located in Europe
0.2 sq mi (0.5 sq km)

DOWN UNDERWATER

These two scenes of the Great Barrier Reef may seem the same, but there are at least 20 differences between them. Find and circle the differences.
ANSWERS ON PAGE 121

114

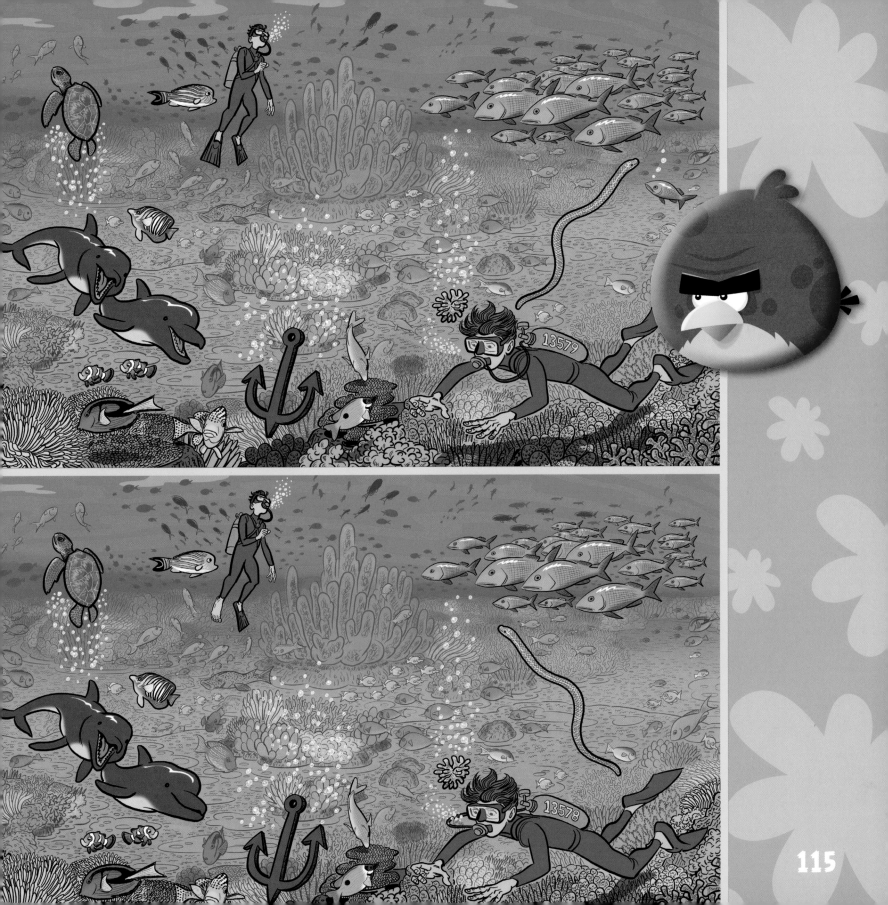

BONUS ACTIVITIES

In this atlas, the Angry Birds have learned a lot about maps and a lot about the world. We've explored the seven different continents with them, visited with people and animals, and seen the natural and human-made wonders of these lands. You and your child can take the lessons they've learned and use them in fun, new experiences that go beyond the pages of this book.

HOUSE ATLAS
(Mapmaking)

The Angry Birds have learned a lot about maps and atlases. Now they're making their own atlas of their home: Piggy Island. You and your child can make an atlas of your home, too! Walk around each room in your home together and make notes of the things that you see. Be sure to include the size and shape of each item. To draw your map, first make an outline of the shape of the room, and then draw each thing about where you saw it. You can also include points of interest and landmarks, such as tables, chairs, refrigerators, bathtubs, stuffed animals—even people! Create a map key with symbols to show what each item is.

CONTINENT COUNT
(Math)

Now that the Angry Birds have learned about maps, they're anxious to count the things they see on them. Help your child join them by turning to the world map on pages 106–107. First, have your child count the continents. As he is counting, he should touch each continent and say the number aloud. Next, count the oceans, touching each name and saying the number aloud. How many continents are there? How many oceans?

A BITE TO EAT
(Observing)
People on each continent produce different kinds of tasty foods. Sometimes the food is eaten right there where it's made, but other times the food is transported and sold in countries on other continents. Your child may not know it, but your pantry and refrigerator may be filled with foods from other lands. Take your child to the grocery store, and observe from which continents and nations certain fruits, vegetables, and other foods originate. Have her take a notebook and write down the different kinds of foods and where they come from. Ask your child where her favorite food is from. Is it your continent, or is it from someplace else? See if she can tell which foods have traveled the farthest to get to you.

GOING TO EXTREMES
(Exercise)
The Angry Birds learned that Earth has a lot of extreme places to explore, such as Mount Everest, the world's tallest mountain, and the Nile, the world's longest river. Lots of people have tried to explore these places. Pretend you and your child are explorers. First, pretend you and your child are mountain climbers scaling Mount Everest. Move your legs and arms as if you were climbing. Ask your child to imagine what it's like on the mountain. Is it cold or hot? What kinds of animals are there? After you get to the top, next pretend that you are exploring the Nile. Move your arms and legs like you're swimming. Have your child talk about the

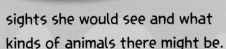
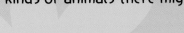

sights she would see and what kinds of animals there might be.

WHAT LIFE IS LIKE
(Storytelling)
The Angry Birds saw how the people of the world live in many different kinds of places, such as mountains, coastlines, deserts, and forests. People's lives can be very different from each other, depending on where they live. Ask your child to use his imagination to write a story about two children, each living in a different kind of place.

Help your child shape his story by asking questions: What are the children's names? What countries are they from? What is the weather like where they live? What kinds of clothes do they wear? Do they eat different foods? Have him describe the weather and what kinds of animals live there.

CLOUD ATLAS

(Observation)

The seven continents have very distinctive shapes, from massive Asia to little Australia. Look up at the sky with your child and watch the clouds. Ask your child if any of the shapes look like countries or continents. What other shapes do they see?

IT'S A SMALL WORLD AFTER ALL

(Music)

The Angry Birds love all the different kinds of music in the world. In Asia, Japanese Taiko drums are a favorite traditional type of music. In North America, Mexican mariachi bands bring a joyful sound to any celebration. In Europe, the *oom-pah* sound of German polka music means dancing and fun. Take your child on

a musical tour with this game. First, write these continents on three index cards: "Asia," "North America," and "Europe" and give them to your child. Using your local library or the Internet (YouTube is a good place to look), find examples of the music of polka, Taiko drums, and a mariachi band. Play a clip of each for your child, and tell her where each comes from. Then select a song, play just ten seconds of it, and ask your child to guess where it comes from by holding up the correct continent card. Once she's mastered these three, investigate other styles of music from all over the world to create new rounds for the game.

MOVING RIGHT ALONG

(Exercise)

The world's animals move around in their own distinctive ways. Kangaroos in Australia get around by hop-hop-hopping. Asia's Komodo dragons creep on all fours. Antarctica's Emperor penguins waddle-waddle over the icy lands. Have your child imagine being each one, moving her body the way each of these animals does.

COLORFUL CONTINENTS

(Art)

Like the Angry Birds themselves, the world is a rainbow of people, places, and things that come in many different colors. Look through the pages on each continent with your child to see what objects you can find in each of these colors: red, orange, yellow, green, blue, purple, brown, black, and white. Make a list of what you find, and see which continent is the most colorful.

MATCH A BIRD

(Memory)

All the world's continents have birds on them, and the Angry Birds learned about at least one bird from each place. To test their memories, they like to play a matching game. To create your own matching game, you'll need 14 index cards and some glue. Help your child find images of each of these birds: bald eagle (North America), scarlet macaw (South America), owl (Europe), penguin (Africa), peacock (Asia), emu (Australia), and Antarctic shag (Antarctica). Print two copies of each bird picture and then paste each one to the back of an index card. Mix up the cards, and then place them face down. On each turn, you and your child turn over two cards to try to make a match. The player with the most matches wins!

CONTINENT CONNECTIONS

(Geography)

The seven continents are huge pieces of land that cover the Earth. Have your child look closely at the world map and ask him to see if any of the continents are connected by land. Can he see which continents touch each other, and which ones stand alone? Ask your child to see what kinds of land features are in between the continents and what kinds of bodies of water separate them.

SIZE MATTERS

(Comparison)

The Angry Birds come in a lot of different sizes—from great big Terence to the little Blues, and everyone in between. The continents come in different sizes, too. Help your child sort

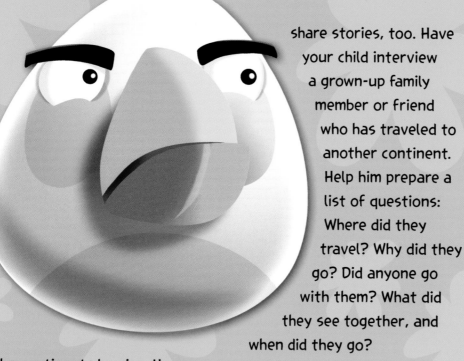

the continents by size. Have her look at the world map on pages 106–107 and touch the continents in order from biggest to smallest, saying the name of each continent as it is touched. Next, try going from smallest to biggest. Check the list on page 110 to see if you've got it right.

SHARING STORIES
(Communication)
When the Angry Birds travel, they love to share the stories of their adventures. People love to share stories, too. Have your child interview a grown-up family member or friend who has traveled to another continent. Help him prepare a list of questions: Where did they travel? Why did they go? Did anyone go with them? What did they see together, and when did they go?

LAND FEATURES
(Art)
Each continent has different types of land features, such as mountains, canyons, lakes, rivers, deserts, grasslands, and rain forests. All of these features look very different from each other. On printer or construction paper, draw these different kinds of environments with your child, using this atlas for visual guidance. Ask her how these places are different and how they are the same. As you're drawing, call out the different colors, shapes, lines, and textures found in each kind of place.

WORLD TRAVELER GUESSING GAME
(Deduction)
Being a world traveler means you get to see lots of cool people, places, and things. Play this guessing game with your child to recall all the amazing things you and the Angry Birds saw in this atlas. Have your child be the World Traveler first, and ask him to think of an animal, place, or thing from one of his "trips" to different continents. He could choose a country, a city, a building, a natural feature—anything mentioned in this book! After he has made a choice, try to guess what it is by asking him questions that can be answered only by "Yes" or "No." Once you guess correctly, it's your turn to be the next World Traveler.

120

READING PASSPORT

(Reading Craft)

Many travelers have a little book called a passport that is stamped whenever they travel from country to country. The stamps help travelers keep track of the places they have been. Before your next trip to the library, create a Reading Passport for your child to help her keep track of the books she's read about other countries. Take several pieces of printer paper and one piece of construction paper. Place the construction paper on the bottom and fold the pile in half. Place three staples along the fold at the top, middle, and bottom to hold it together. Write "Reading Passport" on the front cover, and then glue a picture of your child on the first page. Use the following pages to give your child a stamp and list the books she's read about different countries.

ANSWERS

GO ON SAFARI! (PAGES 112-113)

DOWN UNDERWATER (PAGES 114-115)

GLOSSARY

Not sure what all those words mean? Check out the definitions of some of the most common words you'll find in an atlas.

CAPITAL
The city or town where a country's government is located

CITY
A place where lots of people live; larger than a town or village

CONTINENT
One of the big divisions of land on Earth. There are seven continents: North America, South America, Europe, Africa, Asia, Australia, and Antarctica.

COUNTRY
A place that has a name, boundaries, a flag, and a government that is the highest authority over the land and people who live there

DESERT
A region of Earth with dry lands, few plants, and little rain

GLACIER
A huge, slow-moving mass of ice; glaciers that cover massive areas are called ice caps

GOVERNMENT
The group of people who control and protect a country, state, or city

IMMIGRANTS
People who move from their homeland to live in another country

ISLAND
Land surrounded by water

LAKE
A large body of water surrounded by land

MAP
A drawing of places as they appear from above

MOUNTAIN
A big land feature that rises very high above the land surrounding it

NORTH POLE
The northernmost point on Earth

OCEAN
One of the four large bodies of salt water that cover the Earth

PLAINS
Large areas of mainly flat land, often covered with grasses; also called grasslands

POPULATION
The number of people living in a certain area

RAIN FOREST
A tropical jungle with tall trees that receives at least 100 inches (254 cm) of rain each year

RIVER
A large, natural stream of moving water

SOUTH POLE
The southernmost point on Earth

INDEX

Boldface indicates illustrations.

CREDITS

Published by the National Geographic Society
John M. Fahey, Chairman of the Board and Chief Executive Officer
Declan Moore, Executive Vice President; President, Publishing and Travel
Melina Gerosa Bellows, Executive Vice President; Chief Creative Officer, Books, Kids, and Family

Prepared by the Book Division
Hector Sierra, Senior Vice President and General Manager
Nancy Laties Feresten, Senior Vice President, Kids Publishing and Media
Jennifer Emmett, Vice President, Editorial Director, Children's Books
Eva Absher-Schantz, Design Director, Kids Publishing and Media
Jay Sumner, Director of Photography, Kids Publishing and Media
R. Gary Colbert, Production Director
Jennifer A. Thornton, Director of Managing Editorial

Staff for This Book
Becky Baines, Senior Editor
Amy Briggs, Project Editor
Lori Epstein, Senior Photo Editor
Dawn Ripple McFadin, Designer
Annette Kiesow, Photo Editor
Ariane Szu-Tu, Editorial Assistant

Callie Broaddus, Design Production Assistant
Hillary Moloney, Associate Photo Editor
Carl Mehler, Director of Maps
Sven M. Dolling and Michael McNey, Map Research and Production
Grace Hill, Associate Managing Editor
Joan Gossett, Production Editor
Lewis R. Bassford, Production Manager
Susan Borke, Legal and Business Affairs

Rovio Entertainment Ltd.
Sanna Lukander, Vice President of Book Publishing
Mari Elomäki, Project Editor
Pekka Laine, Project Editor
Jan Schulte-Tigges, Art Director

Production Services
Phillip L. Schlosser, Senior Vice President
Chris Brown, Vice President, NG Book Manufacturing
George Bounelis, Vice President, Production Services
Nicole Elliott, Manager
Rachel Faulise, Manager
Robert L. Barr, Manager

To my baby daughter, Eleanora, and the lifetime of adventures we'll share as we travel the world together. —EC

The National Geographic Society is one of the world's largest nonprofit scientific and educational organizations. Founded in 1888 to "increase and diffuse geographic knowledge," the Society's mission is to inspire people to care about the planet. It reaches more than 400 million people worldwide each month through its official journal, *National Geographic,* and other magazines; National Geographic Channel; television documentaries; music; radio; films; books; DVDs; maps; exhibitions; live events; school publishing programs; interactive media; and merchandise. National Geographic has funded more than 10,000 scientific research, conservation, and exploration projects and supports an education program promoting geographic literacy.

For more information, please visit www.nationalgeographic.com, call 1-800-NGS LINE (647-5463), or write to the following address:
National Geographic Society
1145 17th Street N.W.
Washington, D.C. 20036-4688 U.S.A.

Visit us online at nationalgeographic.com/books

For librarians and teachers: ngchildrensbooks.org

More for kids from National Geographic: kids.nationalgeographic.com

For information about special discounts for bulk purchases, please contact National Geographic Books Special Sales: ngspecsales@ngs.org

For rights or permissions inquiries, please contact National Geographic Books Subsidiary Rights: ngbookrights@ngs.org

Hardcover ISBN: 978-1-4263-1400-1
Reinforced Library Binding ISBN: 978-1-4263-1401-8

Printed in the United States of America
13/CK-CML/1